Bryan Tyson

The Institution of Slavery in the Southern States

Religiously and morally considered in connection with our sectional

troubles

Bryan Tyson

The Institution of Slavery in the Southern States
Religiously and morally considered in connection with our sectional troubles

ISBN/EAN: 9783337255336

Printed in Europe, USA, Canada, Australia, Japan

Cover: Foto ©Andreas Hilbeck / pixelio.de

More available books at **www.hansebooks.com**

THE INSTITUTION OF SLAVERY

IN

THE SOUTHERN STATES,

RELIGIOUSLY AND MORALLY CONSIDERED

IN CONNECTION WITH

OUR SECTIONAL TROUBLES,

BY

BRYAN TYSON

OF NORTH CAROLINA.

———◆———

WASHINGTON, D. C.
H. POLKINHORN, PRINTER, D STREET, BETWEEN 6TH AND 7TH.

1863.

THE INSTITUTION OF SLAVERY

IN

THE SOUTHERN STATES,

RELIGIOUSLY AND MORALLY CONSIDERED

IN CONNECTION WITH

OUR SECTIONAL TROUBLES,

BY

BRYAN TYSON.

OF NORTH CAROLINA.

WASHINGTON, D. C.

H. POLKINHORN, PRINTER, D STREET, BETWEEN 6TH AND 7TH.

1863.

THE INSTITUTION OF SLAVERY

IN THE

SOUTHERN STATES.

IS IT RIGHT OR IS IT WRONG?

But few subjects have been discussed with more interest, and, perhaps, none upon which greater diversity of opinion prevails, than the institution of slavery in the Southern States. Some argue that the institution is just and lawful, having been instituted under a Theocracy; others that it is unjust, inhumane, and ought to be abolished. One or the other of these positions is right and the contrary is wrong. God is on one side or the other of the question, and is opposed to the opposite.

It is now my purpose to inquire impartially into this matter in order, if possible, to determine which side of the question God and justice is on; and should we be so fortunate as to find a solution for the problem, it would then be an easy matter to determine which way the question should be decided.

It may, perhaps, be said that this is not a proper time to discuss this question, but I think never a better. I think a question that has caused so much trouble and distress as this should be discussed, and discussed freely, with an honest search after truth, rather than for the mastery, in order that it may be determined and settled in accordance with the word and justice of God, and settled forever. After our present troubles shall have been ended I hope our country will never again be agitated by this most distressing question.

I will first take the affirmative side of the question, and show wherein it would be best for the servants to remain as they are. Then the negative, or arguments in favor of emancipation. And will then, in conclusion, compare the two together.

Whether or not slavery be right, certain it is that it has existed in all ages from the days of Noah, when a curse was laid upon Canaan, down to the present time. This, I presume, is a conceded fact, and I will, therefore, consume no time in proving this point, it being my object to prove the justness or unjustness of the institution, rather than to prove that it has existed for a long or short period of time.

According to my knowledge of the Old and New Testaments, being an earthly servant here does not appear to be a matter of so very great importance if so be that we are so fortunate as to gain eternal life in the world to come.

We find the word servant mentioned in the Scriptures some four hundred and thirty-five times. This word, however, has different meanings according to the sense in which it is used, but I will mention only a few of these texts, such as are calculated to elucidate the subject under consideration; by far the greater portion having no bearing upon the subject whatever.

We find the word servant mentioned in at least twelve places as pertaining to those that were held to involuntary service or labor. The first place that the word servant is mentioned in the Bible is, I believe, at Genesis, IX, 25, where Noah, awaking from his wine, lays a curse upon Canaan, saying: "cursed be Canaan; a servant of servants shall he be unto his brethren." Soon after this we find by comparing Genesis 10, 2, with Ezekiel 27, 13, that Javan, Tubal and Meshech were trading among them upon the persons of men as merchandise. If this had been wrong it is reasonable to suppose that the practice would have been condemned by the good men of that day. But we do not find it thus condemned. The curse having been pronounced of Noah by inspiration, this was very probably a means devised for carrying it into effect. The sentence "a servant of servants he should be unto his brethren" was irrevocable and was bound to go into effect, let the private opinions of the people of that day have been what they might. It should therefore be the duty of the people in all ages to obey the commands of God, and perform the duties assigned them, rather than to cavil at his decrees, for it is evident that God who made the world can best govern it, and He may also, perhaps, have some object in view not known to us. Therefore we should submit to His commands and decrees. If we would always do this we would be apt to do well enough—better, perhaps, than many of us do.

I can notice but one or two other texts. We will first look at 1 Peter, 2, 18, 21:

"Servants, be subject to your masters with all fear; not only to the good and gentle, but also to the froward.

For this is thank-worthy, if a man for conscience toward God endure grief, suffering wrongfully.

For what glory is it, if, when ye be buffeted for your faults, ye shall take it patiently? but if, when ye do well, and suffer for it, ye take it patiently, this is acceptable with God.

For even hereunto were ye called: because Christ also suffered for us, leaving us an example, that ye should follow his steps."

In the foregoing, servants were plainly commanded to be obedient to their masters, not only to the good and gentle, but also to the froward. And it is evident if a servant who suffers wrongfully and takes it patiently, thereby renders. himself acceptable with God, that it should be the duty of the servant so treated to take it patiently in order that he may render himself acceptable with God.

In the last verse it says: "For even hereunto were ye

called : because Christ also suffered for us, leaving us an example, that ye should follow his steps." Christ was scourged,
mocked, spit upon and crucified, not for his sins, but for the
sins of others, all of which he took patiently. Therefore,
when a servant suffers wrongfully and takes it patiently, he
is but following the example of his blessed Lord and Master.

We will now look at 1 Timothy, 6 ; 1-10 :

"Let as many servants as are under the yoke count their
own masters worthy of all honor, that the name of God and
His doctrine be not blasphemed.

And they that have believing masters, let them not de-
spise them, because they are brethren ; but rather do them
service, because they are faithful and beloved, partakers of
the benefit. These things teach and exhort.

If any man teach otherwise, and consent not to wholesome
words, even the words of our Lord Jesus Christ, and to the
doctrine which is according to godliness ;

He is proud, knowing nothing, but doting about questions
and strifes of words, whereof cometh envy, strife, railings,
evil surmisings.

Perverse disputings of men of corrupt minds, and destitute
of the truth, supposing that gain is godliness : from such
withdraw thyself.

But godliness with contentment is great gain.

For we brought nothing into this world, and it is certain
we can carry nothing out.

And having food and raiment, let us be therewith content.

But they that will be rich fall into temptation and a snare,
and into many foolish and hurtful lusts, which drown men
in destruction and perdition.

For the love of money is the root of all evil : which while
some coveted after, they have erred from the faith, and
pierced themselves through with many sorrows."

For lack of time and space, I will make no comment
whatever on the above text, but will leave it for the reflect-

ing reader to determine for himself, hoping he will give it a careful perusal.

Many things take place in this world that may not appear just and right unto us, but at the same time, God may perhaps have some object in view not known to us. Thus, when Saul was commanded to go and smite the Amelekites, he was commanded to smite every man, woman and child. Even the innocent suckling that had of itself known no guile, was doomed to death.

We are told in another place that God is a jealous God, visiting the iniquities of the fathers upon the children of the third and fourth generations of them that hate Him. Thus it seems we belong to God, and He hath a right to do as seemeth well both with our lives and liberties also. This is exemplified in his works of the smaller creation. If we turn our attention to the beasts of the forest we behold the more ferocious and formidable preying upon the weaker and lesser. If we turn our attention to the fowls of the air we there behold certain species armed with formidable talons, and supplied with carnivorous appetites, and every way fitted by nature for preying upon the weaker and lesser. And if we turn our attention to the fishes of the mighty deep we there behold the same thing. So in very nearly all of God's animate creation, except man, we behold the stronger species preying upon the weaker and lesser. These do not prey merely upon the liberties of the under species, but actually upon their lives, generally inflicting painful and excruciating deaths. So we find that the lives of one class are continually being offered up to support those of the stronger and more ferocious. Even so among men, so far as liberty is concerned, we find the superior, more intelligent and gifted by nature, preying upon the weaker and less intelligent, in reducing them to bondage, and compelling them to serve their superiors. This, no doubt, appears revolting to the feelings of any christian, humane man ; but the institution of slavery has now got a foot-hold among us. The people of this generation are by no means responsible for this class of people being reduced to bondage. Therefore it becometh our duty as philanthropists, to study their case, and do by them what is best under ex-isting circumstances, such as we would like to have done unto us under similar circumstances. I will treat of this more at length before I get through.

But says one, the servitude spoken of in the Scriptures is applicable only to the Hebrews, the command having been given especially to them, and therefore we have no right to hold servants under that command unless we can establish that we are of Hebrew descent. I will acknowledge that there is some feasibility in this argument; and not wishing to lay any burden upon these people, not even so large as my little finger, I will not argue the question any farther in that light, nor will I take any advantage of the curse laid upon Canaan, but will proceed to argue it solely in a moral point of view, being not only willing but anxious that the question may be decided according to the best interests of the servants, be it which way it may. Because, admitting that the Scriptures would permit us to hold or own servants, there is no law nor obligation that I know of that would compel or bind us as our duty to hold them. And believ-ing it to be unjust that one part of the human race should be deprived of their liberty and happiness in order to in-crease the happiness of another class, I think the interests of servants should be consulted exclusively in this matter, and let them be emancipated or remain as they are, according as their interests require. I will now proceed to argue this question in a moral point of view.

We will first look at this institution in a family where there are some thirty or forty servants. We find among them a good many women and children, and some old men and women who are not able to do regular field labor. So out of the whole we will probably not get more than four-ninths who are regular field hands. The children play about at their sports—the white and black almost invariably together, where there are children of each kind on a place—until they reach a proper age to put to work, which is light at first, but, as they grow older, gradually assumes a heavier form until they get so that they can do any work that is done on the farm. Their labor is now of some value, and a part of it goes towards supporting the women and children and the old men and women who are now too old to labor. They thus continue to labor, and in the course of time declining years set in and they too cease to be any longer regular field hands. They are now assigned some light work, such as boiling food and feeding stock, looking after and training the children, &c. The young negroes that they helped to raise, now, in turn, labor to support them in their declining years. So it appears to be one continuous copartnership, as it were, they having all things common, like as is described in the fourth chapter of the Acts of the Apostles. The children, when they are too young to labor, likewise when they get to be too old, fare equally as well as when they were at a proper age to labor. Thus, of the three stages—youth, middle age, and old age—through which servants pass, there is but one in which they are depended on as regular field hands. In old age they are taken good care of; and thus is the entire slave population rendered self-supporting. So, of the 3,953,760 that were in the United States in 1860, I don't suppose there was one of that number supported by public tax. Such an instance, I presume, is unknown among an equal number of industrial classes any where in the civilized world. If there has been any property accumulated from the labor of the servant during his younger days, that very same property stands pledged to take care of him in old age. I will ask where else on the face of the globe could you go to find, in a population of nearly four millions, no paupers?

TREATMENT OF SERVANTS.

The servants at the South, for the most part, receive good treatment, as is evident from the census returns of 1860. During that year there were 3,000 servants manumitted, and 803 escaped to the North as fugitives, making a total loss to the slave population of 3,803. Taking this as the annual loss for the past decade, there would thus have been a loss to the slave population of 38,030. But, with this odds against them, the slave population at the South increased during the decade ending in 1860, 23.39 per cent.; which is faster than any nation in Europe increased during the same period of time. The free blacks during the same period, after having been augmented by about 38,030, increased only 12.33 per cent.

I will here give the statistics of some of the principal northern cities. In the city of Boston, during the five years ending in 1859, the city register observes: "The number of colored births was one less than the number of marriages, and the deaths exceeded the marriages nearly in the proportion of two to one. In Philadelphia, during the last six months of the census year, the new city registration gives 148 births against 306 deaths among the free colored people. So we find that the slaves or servants of the South, notwithstanding they were subject to two considerable drains as aforesaid, increased nearly as fast again as their free brethren. From this we would infer that the better treatment was in favor of the bond servant. This, I think, is the effect of their working in societies or copartnership as already explained. For thus situated, the women at times, when their health is delicate, are not required to labor, being taken about as good care of as a member of the white family under similar circumstances. I have known the owner, in cases where a large percentage of his servants were women and children, to have to labor himself very hard, and always have his nose down to the grinstone in order to raise these children, while they were running about, kicking up their heels, and seeing their pleasure. But they were willing to undergo this toil, with the hope that they would be able to pay for their raising some time.

The servants at the South are not only, generally speaking, well treated, but becoming respect is also shown them in old age. The white children are even taught to call the elderly servants uncle or aunt, as the case may be. I was thus brought up myself, and it still appears natural for me to do so.

Where servants are properly and well treated, I think they frequently fare better, and have more of the necessaries and comforts of life to go upon than many of the poorer class of white people; and the reason of this is, they attend more systematically to business; for while the voice of the former is heard loud and long. at the tavern, or other places of amusement, these are attending to their daily avocations which furnish food and raiment for the body and employment for the mind; and being thus employed, they are kept out of mischief.

I think the unexampled increase among the servants is owing to the society or copartnership in which they live, together with the early age at which they generally marry. (I will speak of the mode presently.) In making matches, there are no questions of a worldly character to decide with them; for their women are all like Lycurgus would have those of Sparta, all equal as to property.

Among various laws that this learned sage introduced into Sparta was one that females should inherit no part of their father's estate, but that it should be equally divided among his sons. Being called upon to explain the object of this curious law he said, the young men in making matches would not then be picking and choosing after property, but would go for worth and merit. It also seems that some such a law would have an excellent effect in this day and time in

encouraging early marriages and thus prevent the unnatural state of celibacy, with its many concurrent evils, for
where people marry for wealth and character, they frequently
keep picking and choosing after these until they pick
through and get nobody. Therefore, under a discipline that
would cause early and universal marriages, religion, morals,
and school-houses would doubtless flourish.

The servants generally live up to this rule ; for there being no questions of a worldly character to decide with them,
they go in solely for " love and beauty." The consequence
is, there are but few or no cases of celibacy among them ;
they have but few or no cares as to their rising families,
and in old age they are taken good care of. So, where they
are properly and well treated, they are, in my opinion, about
the happiest people the sun shines on.

ENJOYMENT OF SERVANTS.

In order that the reader may have some idea of the manner in which servants enjoy themselves, I will relate the following incident :

The past summer, a year ago, I was at a friend's house in
Chatham county, North Carolina, who owned a good many
servants. It was in time of wheat harvest. About dusk the
hands came in from their laborious work. It would seem
that all might have been tired enough without seeking farther exercise in diversions, but not so. After supper the
banjo was brought forth, and preparations made for a social
dance. They soon struck up in high glee. I remarked to
my friend that negroes saw a great deal of satisfaction and
pleasure. Yes, said he, the most of any people in this
world. He told me that wishing to finish a certain field of
grain, they had labored very hard that day. But one would
not have judged so from present appearances. When I
went to bed they were in the midst of their glee, making
the house fairly shake as their busy feet kept time to the

music. So in what position in life could they be more happy? We should not form the belief because they have to labor that they are rendered unhappy; for the Bible, I think says: "The repose of the laboring man is sweet." They have to labor or their owners would soon be reduced to a condition such as to be unable to treat them well. Hence we may conclude if they be placed in a position where idleness would be encouraged, that their condition, instead of being bettered, would thereby be worsted. For, as the saying is, "when idleness comes in at one door, want, with crime and its various attendants, come in at another." But servants, for the most part, live free from these evils, and are, therefore, a contented and happy people.

FREE NEGROES VOLUNTARILY ENSLAVE THEMSELVES.

At all events, the felicity of the bond servant is such that I have actually known free persons of color to choose their masters and voluntarily enslave themselves. This may appear very singular to us, but unless they expected to better their condition, it is still more strange that they should thus voluntarily give away their liberty. It is to be presumed that they considered the matter well before entering into this engagement. But, inheriting by birth no wealth, and not being able to amass means sufficient, above the necessary expenses of life, to purchase lands, horses, &c., and thus put themselves in a comfortable situation for living, it seems that, rather than weary thus with the burdens of life, and hire themselves from house to house, and be dependent on uncertain means, they had rather pick out some good, kind, humane man for a master, who was well supplied with all the necessaries and comforts of life, and who they knew would treat them well, than to have their liberty and thus be taxed with the cares and concerns of life. After trying their new homes I never heard of any dissatisfaction on their part; so it is to be presumed they were satisfied with the change.

EFFECTS OF EMANCIPATION.

To show the effect of emancipation on these people, I refer the reader to the history of Jamaica, Hayti and British Guiana, countries where emancipation has taken place. In these countries the negroes invariably ceased to work to much advantage after gaining their freedom. To prove this I will mention a few facts.

In the year 1790 there was exported from the Island of Hayti 163,405,220 pounds sugar. After gaining their freedom the quantity began to diminish, and in forty-three years thereafter there was not a single pound exported from the Island, and the Queen Island of the seas was thus relinquished to barbarism, desolation, brutal licentiousness and crime, in every hideous form. I could multiply these instances, but, wishing to be brief, will let the above suffice.

It is said that bees when transported to the Island of Cuba soon cease to work and lay up honey, and divert themselves by flying about the sugar mills and stinging the hands whilst at work. The reason that they thus cease to labor is that they can always get a sufficiency of the necessary food without being at that trouble. Past experience has generally proven this to be the case with the negro where he has been emancipated—he soon ceases to work to much advantage.

THE NEGRO CAN LABOR WITH IMPUNITY AMONG VARIOUS EPIDEMIC DISEASES.

It seems the negro should not be entirely idle, because he is well adapted for laboring on the cotton, rice and sugar plantations of the South, and can labor with impunity among various epidemic diseases where the white man would soon sicken and die. To prove this I refer to the following:

In the summer of 1855, during that awful scourge of yellow fever in Norfolk, Va., there died in that city about 3,000 persons. Of these there were but very few cases among the blacks. I was there for a considerable time among the fever myself, and I know I heard it remarked that it took but little or no effect on the black population. So they seem to be well adapted for working on the cotton, rice and sugar plantations of the South, in which the North, South, and various European countries are interested. In warm countries, where serpents and alligators abound, there the negro flourishes to greatest perfection. But remove him from this to a Northern clime and he soon shows unmistakable signs of decay. It is therefore evident that his labor is particularly essential in rearing the tropical products, and experience has taught, that to raise these successfully, he requires the aid and superveilance of the white man.

ARGUMENTS AGAINST SLAVERY.

I will now notice the negative side of the question and proceed to give the arguments that are generally brought against the institution of slavery.

Among the first and principal of these is the enhanced value of real estate in the Free States and the prevailing ignorance among the poorer classes South when compared with their Northern brethren. We will notice these arguments separately. In 1850 the average value of land in the Northeen States was, I believe, $28.07 per acre. In the Southern, $5.34 per acre. But is this high price in the one case and low in the other attributable solely to the institution of slavery at the South? I think not. I think it is mainly owing to the very dense population of the Northern States and the more sparse or scattering of the Southern, together with the system of trade that has been carried on between the two sections. Thus, the people at the South have nearly forty-five acres of land per head, counting both black and white, great and small. The people at the North have less than twenty-one. So we should not wonder that lands are higher at the North, because scarcity always enhances the value of anything. It should also be recollected that city property, manufactories, &c., are counted in the above estimate; and the Northern States having larger cities and more manufactories than the Southern States, have greatly the advantage in this particular.

If we compare the Northwestern with the Southwestern States we shall find the average value of land in the North western to be $11 39 per acre; in the Southwestern $6 26. So the lands of the Southwestern people are worth more per head than those of the Northwestern; for what they lack in price they more than make up in the number of acres.

But after all, is the enhanced or high price of land any advantage to the generality of people? I think not; no more than the selling of corn at five dollars per bushel would be to the buyer. Where lands are cheap the poor can buy them and every man own his tract of land; but placed at these enormously high prices, the rich alone can afford to be landholders.

As regards the superior intelligence of the masses of the people North compared with the masses South, I think that is mainly attributable to the system of trade that has been carried on between the Northern and Southern States, together with, perhaps, the better system with which schools have been conducted in the Free States. It is said that the South, poor as she is, has annually poured into the lap of the North about $230,000,000 This amount of money expended among the Northern people was calculated to make everything flourishing. Their manufactured articles all commanding ready sales, they could, with the proceeds thereof, school their children and do almost anything else they desired, whilst at the South the people, banks, and everything else were languishing under this murderous system of trade. Had the necessary manufactories been built up at the South, and these $230,000,000 been expended annually among the poorer classes there, they too, I presume, would have been able to educate their children, and business of every kind would soon have been in a thriving and prosperous condition. But after all, I am inclined to think that the superiority of the Northern people, in a literary point of view, compared with their Southern brethren, is not as great as has commonly been supposed. And as regards morals, I have it from reliable statistics that the religious persons South, according to population, exceed those North nearly in the proportion of two to one. So it seems what they lack in learning, if any, they make up in religion.

A LARGE AMOUNT OF NORTHERN PROFITS DERIVED FROM SOUTHERN LABOR.

Let the institution of slavery have been what it might, it is evident that the Northern people got the sum and substance of it, while the Southern people got the shadow. The tide of trade had got turned to the North to such a degree that articles of Southern manufacture would scarcely sell; or at least the Northern was generally prefered as they were thought to be a little cheaper. Capitalists were, therefore afraid to invest their money in these enterprises, for it was evident without the benefit of the Southern trade they could not be sustained.

I will give an example of this. There were, in a certain small county in one of the Southern States, (Randolph, North Carolina,) five large and flourishing cotton manufactories, all being upon the same water course. These factories turned out large amounts of cloth and thread, but supplying none but the home market, they soon became overstocked with these goods, and in order to find sale for them, large quantities had to be sent to the Northern markets, principally New York, where they came in competition with the goods of Northern and various European manufacturers. Now, in order to find sale for these goods, they could not be offered at a price higher than the Northern and European could be bought at. But, the profits of the Southern manu-

2

facturer being materially lessened by the expense of transportation, commissions, &c., what do you suppose was the consequence of this murderous system of trade ? Why, several of these manufacturing companies soon failed to meet their demands, and some of the stockholders, who not happening to have a surplus of means, had to sell their stock at a reduced price in order to meet their demands. So, with this prospect of things before the Southern people, it is not to be wondered at that they were afraid to risk their capital in manufacturing enterprises. The institution of slavery cannot, I presume, be brought as an argument against the want of success of these factories, because they were all operated exclusively by white hands. Nor can it be said that the Southern people were not able to sustain them, for they had means in abundance to do this, but these were, generally speaking, sent North. Their failure, then, was simply owing to lack of home patronage.

But soon after the Northern trade was broken up by our sectional troubles, these same goods advanced in value over 500 per cent. Many of the manufacturing companies throughout the South doubled the wages to their hands and still made enormous profits. If this state of things had taken place in time of peace, these enhanced prices would have caused other manufactories to spring up, and thus, in time, these goods, through competition, would have been brought down sufficiently low. Employment would then have been given to our poorer classes, and under these circumstances all would have journeyed on prosperously and happily together. I think we would then have been able to show our Northern brethren that the presence of a few niggers at the South could not keep us from manufacturing nor from doing anything else we wished to do. I desire to see the whole country prosper, both the North and the South, and for this purpose I think they should trade together as far as such trading would be of mutual advantage to each other. But

I am not in favor of this trade being carried to such an extent as to enrich one section and impoverish the other, and then lay all the fault to the existence of a certain institution in one of the sections, while they themselves received a large amount of their profits from this same institution. I will endeavor to make this a little plainer by giving a fable that very probably the reader is familiar with:

THE ASS, THE LION AND THE COCK.

Once upon a time there was a lion that espied an ass at a distance feeding, and having a mind to make his dinner off of her, he began to creep slowly toward the ass, with the intention of making her his prey. But just before he should give the fatal spring the cock crew. The lion, having a great antipathy to the crowing of the cock, turned about and scampered away as fast as possible. The ass, thinking that the lion was fleeing from her, turned and pursued after, and would every now and then feed him in the side with her heels. They kept on thus until the lion got the ass off as far as he desired, when he turned round and accomplished his first desire, which was to make his dinner off of her.

Even so with the Northern people. Vast heaps of wealth having concentrated in the Northern States, it has, I fear, caused our Northern brethren to become a little arrogant and presumptious, thinking it was their superior skill and shrewdness that has caused this great concentration of wealth. But in very many instances the source of this same wealth is mainly attributable to the labor of Southern servants, whom so many of our Northern brethren are now chasing with a desire of changing his social position. But even if they succeed, mind you if they too, in the end, like the ass, will not suffer most by it.

If I had time and space I could trace this subject further and show that the panics that have been occurring in our money markets at the South, at intervals of a few years for a good many years back, were mainly attributable to the South overtrading with the North and the North overtrading with Europe; but I will leave this part of the subject with the reflecting reader.

A FEW QUESTIONS TO BE ANSWERED.

I will here ask the emancipationists a question, and that is, if there be such an advantage in free labor over slave, why does not the people of England, Scotland, Ireland and other countries of Europe enjoy this to the same extent that the people of the Northern States have done? This question can be easily answered. In the first place the Free States are not so densely populated as those countries; and in the second place they have not had such a place to trade and draw their supplies from as the Northern States. But if the South would produce less of the raw material, and become to a certain extent a manufacturing people, mind you if the scale would not soon turn. Soon after the discovery of the cotton gin, cotton commanding very high prices, the Southern people became alive to producing the raw material. The climate of the North not being adapted to the growing of cotton, they erected the necessary manufactories and became a manufacturing people. Their goods too commanding high prices, soon increased their capital, which enabled them to build more manufactories. The Northern people having got their manufactories in successful operation, it would now be impossible for manufactories to be built up at the South, without affording them some protection in their infancy. And all the protection they would require would be for the Southern people to patrouize them, let the price be high or low. In time, competition would bring all things right, as has already been stated.

The people of the Northern States boast of the rapidity with which their new States have grown up. This is owing to the emigration from Europe and other countries. But when these States shall have become as thickly settled as those European countries, in what particular will they possess an advantage over the people of those countries? I answer, in nothing, unless they have the benefit of the Southern trade.

NUMBER OF PERSONS WHO DO NOT TREAT THEIR SERVANTS WELL COMPARATIVELY SMALL.

Again, it is argued that servants are not properly and well treated; that they are kept in the dark and sometimes ill-treated also. This is even so, and I desire to see improvement in both cases.

As regards evil treatment I will admit that there are a few who do not treat their servants well, but the number is small in comparison with those who do treat them well. Would you then bring evil upon the whole race merely because there are a few persons who do do not treat their servants well? The time never has been, and probably never will be, when, in a population of nearly four millions of people, whether they be bond or free, that there will not be some acts of violence committed on the weakly and inoffensive.

But in order to remedy these defects, would you entail evil upon the whole race? I think not. I will illustrate this by the following:

Railroads are known to be great conveniences; but still accidents occasionally occur upon them which sometimes result in death. Now in order to remedy these evils, you would not do away with the entire railroad system, would you? No, I think not. I think you will readily admit that the good accomplished by them more than overbalances the evil.

But suppose a servant is harshly treated; that he has fallen into the hands of a hard taskmaster. In this case let him raise his petition to Christ, who is no respector of persons, and justice will eventually be done. I have thought if there be an earthly temple fit for the Spirit of Christ to dwell in that it is a servant who is evily treated. God, in His infinite wisdom, did not intend that justice should be meted out in this world. If He had, there would be no need of a judgment in the next. Therefore, if the servant evily treated will raise his petition to Him who ruleth on high, it will, I think, in the end be of no disadvantage to him. The hard taskmaster will, in a coming day, stand at the bar of God, there to be judged according to the deeds done in the body, and there will be shown no respect of persons.

SERVANTS SHOULD BE TAUGHT TO READ.

I wish to do these people justice throughout, and I, therefore, desire that they should be sent to school, and at least taught to read, so as to be able to read the Scriptures. It has been thought by some emancipationists that such a course would lead to enfranchisement. If it would, I am for it. The soul is evidently of more importance than the body, and should, therefore, be first cared for. I will remark, though, that the best servants I have ever known were such as could read, and were religious. It creates a moral worth in them. But still, should such a course lead to enfranchisement, I am for it as aforesaid. They would then be in a fit condition to take care of themselves. But turn them out in their present ignorant condition, and it is feared disastrous consequences would follow.

MARRIAGE AMONG THE SERVANTS.

It is also argued that the servants at the South live in open adultery, never having been legally married.

In answer to this I will say, that a great many are married after book form; and they all, so far as my knowledge goes, have their choice in this matter, whether to be married after book form or cohabit under a vow. I will take occasion to state here that I believe the essential part of the marriage contract consists in a solemn vow between the parties, and a faithful observance thereof. There being so many different forms of marriage among the various nations of the earth, it is hard to tell which is right. But I am inclined to think that, where the parties cohabit under a solemn vow, and observe it faithfully, whether made privately or publicly, there is no adultery committed. So far as my knowledge goes, the servants that cohabit under a vow are fully as faithful to their companions as those who are married after book form, and in both cases they are generally true to their engagements. But still I am for granting the servants their discretion in this matter, and let all that wish to be married after book form do so. Or if it be found more in accordance with the Word and justice of God that they should be married after book form, I am, if you please, in favor of that, and even of compelling all to be thus wedded. Cohabiting under a vow seems to have been peculiar to ancient days: that of book form or public marriages to modern. So much for marriage among the servants.

AMALGAMATION.

Another argument that is frequently brought against the institution of slavery is the amalgamation of the white and black races. It is true this is an evil. But, it is thought, this could be effectually prevented by passing a simple law in reference thereto; and that is, that all such issues born of white parents on one side, should, as soon as capable of taking care of themselves, or, at farthest, at the age of twenty one years, go out free. In this case, as the owner of servants would not care to raise children who would be of but little or no profit to him, it is to be presumed means would be adopted such as would prevent an increase of this kind among his servants. New cases being thus prevented, the mixed races now on hand would soon become extinct through the largely superior number of pure blacks. As is now the case, amalgamation is most prevalent in towns and cities; but it is thought the above would, in a few generations measurably wipe out the whole, and that the negroes would thenceforth be enabled to maintain their original purity.

SLAVERY THE CAUSE OF THE WAR.

Another argument that is brought against Slavery is, that it is the cause of the present war, and should therefore be abolished. I think in this case our duty as philanthropists, should be to study their case and place them in the position in which they would be most comfortable and happy, and then let the people of each section conform thereto.

BUYING AND SELLING SERVANTS.

Again: It is argued that servants should not be bought and sold, and thus parted from families and relatives. This does seem hard; and unless some one else were more in favor of it than I am there would be but few bought and sold, I assure you. But the principle at last tends to transfer them from a poorer section to one more fertile and congenial; and I doubt not many changes have thus been made by which the condition of servants were bettered, which was not apparent at the time. Thus, I am credibly informed, that in the Southern and Southwestern States a servant frequently makes for himself a bale of cotton in the time given him, which he appropriates to his own private purposes. In a less fertile section, probably in the one from whence he came, he could not do this. This age is one of emigration any way, and how often do we see members of a white family scattered into almost as many States as there are members!

As regards parting a man and wife, and small children from their parents, I am utterly opposed to that. I will remark, though, that in a sojourn at the South of over twenty years, I have known but very few cases where a man and wife were parted. There is a disposition among the people to keep them together as much as possible. But I would be glad to see laws passed at the South to prohibit a man and wife from being separated under any and all circumstances, and such is now the case in some of the States.

FUGITIVE SLAVE LAW.

Another argument which is frequently brought against the institution of slavery—or rather against the rendition of fugitive slaves, which in substance is the same thing—is found at Deut. xxiii, 15, 16: "Thou shalt not deliver unto his master his servant which has escaped from his master unto thee; he shall dwell with thee, even among you in that place which he shall choose in one of the gates where it liketh him best: thou shalt not oppress him."

The above text is capable of a two-fold interpretation: First, that the Hebrews were the only people permitted to own servants. This is verified by their being commanded not to deliver up fugitive servants, they being supposed to have escaped from some of the heathen nations round about. Second, that, as they were commanded not to deliver up these servants, and at the same time were not commanded to interpose so as to keep their masters from recovering them, the text merely means non-interference or neutrality.

I will illustrate this by the following: We will say your ox strays off and gets over on your neighbor's plantation. You miss him and go and search for him, and when you have found him, bring him home without, perhaps, your neighbor knowing that he had been there; he does not deliver him to you.

But if your ox go and get in your neighbor's corn, and he put him up in a stall and send you word, and when you come, he should then show and deliver him unto you, this might be called delivering. Even so in this case. You cannot deliver a servant unto his master unless you are instrumental in his recovery. It would seem that a servant escaping from his master and seeking refuge in a foreign land would be apt to have some just cause for so doing. In this case it would now be very cruel in you to hunt down this servant and be instrumental in any way in again placing him in bondage under his former taskmaster. But if you remain still, and do nothing, neither the one way nor the other, then is the case very different.

It is also argued that the servants should be emancipated, and if the whites need their services let them hire them and pay them wages therefor. The probability is, if they were emancipated their labor could not be commanded, not even for money, or at least not regularly enough for farm purposes; for experience has generally proven that where they have been emancipated they soon get to be like bees when transported to the Island of Cuba—soon cease to work to much advantage, as already stated. It is, therefore, to be presumed that both themselves and cotton fields would soon languish under immediate and thorough emancipation. It should also be borne in mind that the relations existing between a master and his servant are quite different from those existing between the same person and a hired servant. In the one case he is considered and treated as a member of the family; in the other, but little regard is manifested for him after receiving his wages, and he is able to obtain but few favors—only such as he can purchase with his money—which in many instances are fewer than those the bond servant enjoys.

I will here ask the question how much does the richest man in New York get for taking care of his riches? I answer, only what he eats, drinks, and wears. "But they that will be rich fall into temptation and a snare, and into many foolish and hurtful lusts, which drown men in destruction and perdition." Therefore, if thou hast food and raiment, therewith be content.

COMPARISON.

I will now treat of this subject in comparison :

In order to show the effect that religion, light, and the influence that the white man has had on these people, I will give a brief biographical sketch of

A NEGRO PREACHER.

A good many years ago there resided in the county of Moore, North Carolina, a negro whose name was Ralph. He professed religion early in life, and it was soon discovered that he had a gift for the ministry. By assiduous study he soon became learned and mighty in the Scriptures. The church to which he belonged, seeing that he was likely to be useful, contributed, bought, and gave him his freedom. Taking the name of his master, he was known thereafter as Ralph Freeman. He formed an acquaintance with a Baptist minister of the name of McGee. They soon became very intimate, and traveled and preached much together. At length they made an agreement that whoever died first the other should preach his funeral. Soon after this McGee removed to Alabama, where, after several years, he died, leaving his friend Ralph still surviving. In his will he left Ralph his horse, bridle and saddle, overcoat, Bible, and fifty dollars in money, and requested that he should be informed of his decease ; which was accordingly done, and, by agreement, a time set for the preaching of the funeral. A few weeks before the appointed time Ralph, now grey-headed and well stricken in years, set out on his long journey to fulfil the pledge that he had made with his white brother many years before. He reached his place of destination in due time. It being a novel thing that a colored preacher should come from North Carolina to Alabama to preach a funeral, a vast concourse of people assembled on the occasion. To use Ralph's own words, "the whole land of Judea and region round about had come out to hear him." He said, the assemblage of people being so large, he feared he would not be able to realize their expectations. But he said he had not preached far before every bone in the old negro felt like preaching. His discourse was well received, and after services a collection was taken up, and $100 contributed for his benefit. Thus we see what effect light and religion has on these people.

Contrast the above with the following, or negro at home, by M. Jules Gerard, which you may find in the *Philadelphia Inquirer*, of September 7th, 1863:

THE KING OF DAHOMEY.

The following letter has been received by the Duke of Wellington from the celebrated lion-hunter, M. Jules Gerard:

"Monsieur le Duc—Your Grace is well aware that few men gain by being seen close, unless they are men of intellect and merit. The King of Dahomey, despite his cognomen, which signifies the 'Eternal,' or the 'Infinite,' fully justifies that rule, to which he is no exception. Physically he is similar to the other blacks of his country, tall, well built, a head like a bull dog. The most usual expression of his countenance is that of cunning and cruelty. His moral qualities are in perfect keeping with his physical conformation; he is more gracious than the Kings who have preceded him, fanatical for old traditions and customs. The traditions of that microscopic court are to turn the whites to the best possible account (*exploiter les blancs*,) but especially to induce them to make presents. It is the custom to excite the people with sanguinary spectacles, so as to be able to carry off the neighboring population when a slave dealer makes an offer to the King, and also at the annual custom of human sacrifices.

I have just spent twenty days at Kana, where the King was staying for the celebration of the lesser ceremonies. On the day of my presentation I was conducted across the market place, where twelve corpses were exposed to view on separate sites. Six were hung up by the feet; the six others were upright, like men about to walk. Those whom I saw close were horribly mutilated and not beheaded. An enormous pool of blood covered the ground beneath the scaffold, giving unmistakable evidence of previous sacrifices and of the tortures which accompanied them. Our reception by the king was brilliant, very cordial for myself as well as for the French Consul; but we were soon able to convince ourselves that this was but a comedy always performed by this poor Paladin to get the presents brought by the whites. Born and brought up in the midst of these spectacles, which would be ridiculous if they were not horrible, the present

King is actually more fond of them than his subjects. I saw him on that day admiring with the delight of a child the grotesque dances and ridiculous pantomime of his ministers, and then of the princes, and then of all present, for our amusement.

A most infernal music, which nearly deafened us, delighted the King, who seemed to be in a state of ecstacy, and this, M. le Duc, lasted for six hours. On the following day his Majesty invited us to witness a procession of the King's riches. On reaching the square of the Palace (red huts) an agreeable surprise had been prepared for us. The entrance gate was flooded by a pool of blood two yards in width, and on each side a column of recently decapitated heads formed two immense chaplets. It is true that on this day the King wore the emblem of Christ on his breast. It must be presumed that it was the cross of execution that he meant to imply by this ornament. As regards the procession of his wealth, it consisted of a few old carriages, bath chairs carried by men with figures like Polichinello. One thousand women carried each a bottle of liquor on her head ; a brass basin in the shape of a foot-bath to receive the blood of the human victims on the day of the King's banquet ; an image of the Virgin ; various basketsfull of human skulls ; an image of St. Lawrence, as large as life, carried by blacks ; finally the *drum of death.*

At another festival the King commanded on foot his Amazons, who manœuvred with the precision of a flock of sheep. On the market place, already mentioned, each step was ornamented by a dead body ; and the King came and went in the midst of pools of blood and fragments of human flesh in a state of putrifaction. On this occasion he had daubed his face with coal. The ceremony terminated with a mad dance, in which the King took part, dancing *vis-a-vis* to drunken soldiers and musicians. Such are, M. le Duc, the man, the Government and the people whom we have hitherto hoped to turn into a path less contrary to the laws of humanity. I regret that Captain Burton should have arrived at Kana just at the moment of the King's departure, as he might have been enabled to see and judge of all these things.

I am, M le Duc, your most obedient servant,

JULES GERARD.

P. S.—On the day of his departure the King invited us to a review of his army prepared for war. It was from 12,000 to 15,000 strong, comprising 12,000 Amazons, 1,000 men of the body-guard, and 2,000 archers."

We are informed that the Philistines, upon a certain occasion, became masters of the Ark of the Lord, but whilst it was in their possession they were sorely smitten, and could have no peace until the same was returned from whence it came. Even so with the servants. If their being subordinate to the whites were wrong it seems they should be returned to Africa from whence they came, even to the dominions of King Dahomey. But who is it that says the condition of servants would be bettered by such a transposition?

MORALITY OF THE FREE BLACKS AT THE NORTH AND SOUTHERN SERVANTS COMPARED.

In 1850, while there was one colored convict in the penitentiary of Massachusetts for every 192 of her free colored population, there was only one in every 10,000 of the servants at the South in prison. (I here select Massachusetts for a parallel, because the negroes there have enjoyed freedom longer than those of any other State. In some of the other free States crime among the free blacks is even greater than among those of Massachusetts.) But, says one, they are governed and kept in their places by their masters, so that it is not often they are imprisoned, only for some heinous offence. This is even so; and from it we would infer that some special government was needed for the free blacks North, in order to reduce the enormous amount of crime now existing among them to at least a respectable figure.

In Massachusetts there is only 1 in every 109 of her population free negroes. So the proportion being so small, they do not make any great impression on Society. But suppose they all be emancipated at the South and remain among the whites, where in some of the States the number of negroes exceeds the whites, and that they in a few years should become thirteen times as immoral as the whites, what do you think would then be the condition of society there? Consider the matter coolly and deliberately, my reader, and give me a calm, dispassionate answer.

But, any person that has traveled at the South, and noticed things for himself, has doubtless observed that the servants are, generally speaking, a very moral, contented, and happy people, and very many religious also.

FORMER AND PRESENT CONDITION OF EMANCIPATED
SERVANTS COMPARED.

I will now give the experience of some of the lately emancipated servants:

One of these, a negro man, told me in the streets of Newbern, that he was not as free now as he was before he came into
the Federal lines. And also that he fared better particularly
in sickness, for, said he, when I got sick I had some person
to bring medicine out to me; but it is not so now.

I do not mention this in disparagement to the Federal
authorities; for I, doubt not, they have taken as good
care of these people as they could possibly do under
existing circumstances. When we take into consideration
the magnitude of our sectional troubles, and disturbed condition of the country, our great wonder is that they have
been able to do as well by them as they have.

ANOTHER CASE.

A woman that formerly belonged to a gentleman who
owned some three hundred of these people, said she fared
better and was better contented before obtaining her freedom than she had been since. This woman was a hired servant at the house at which I boarded for several weeks
whilst in Newbern. At length, the number of the lady's
boarders not justifying her in keeping so many servants,
she was dismissed, and without means and without employment thrown upon the world to beat her way through life's
uneven way as best she could. "Without means and without employment" will, I fear, be a frequent cry raised by
these people.

ANOTHER CASE.

I will now give the experience of an old colored person
with whom I conversed, at the market-house, in this city,
but a few days ago. He said, a good many years ago, his

master, living in South Carolina, emancipated himself and family, consisting of his wife and seven children—four sons and three daughters—and gave them money to bear their expenses to a free State. He said at first he hailed this change with much joy, as he expected to get aid from his children; but they had all scattered off, his wife was now dead, and he was dependent on his own labor for support, and now, being very old, he was ill able to labor. I asked him which situation he would prefer, to be back with his master, or live the way he was now living? He said his master was a good and kind man, and if he was now back with him he would never consent to leave him again. Said he, I then had some time to rest, but I have none now.

If we contrast the present condition of the servants in the cases just mentioned with their former condition, and take their own word as evidence, how does the matter stand?

I will here remark that I have taken but little pains to inform myself on this subject, having conversed with probably not more than a half-dozen relative thereto, some of whom (I recollect definitely but one) said they were better satisfied since obtaining their freedom than before. These were mostly young, hearty laborers who were then working at good wages. Whether this state of things will continue after the war shall have subsided, and business become stagnant, and particularly after old age shall have set in, I am unable to say. We will, though, take it for granted that what has proven true in a few cases will in very nearly all similarly situated.

I will here ask the question, if these servants who have tried both modes of living say they were better off and lived more comfortably in their former than latter condition. how is it that the emancipationists, who know but comparatively little of the institution of slavery any way, should know so much better what suits them best than the servants do themselves?

THE CONDITION OF BOND SERVANTS AND FREE PERSONS OF COLOR AT THE SOUTH CONTRASTED.

Near where I resided, in North Carolina, there lived a family of free negroes, which consisted of a man and his wife and one or two children, the remaining children having scattered off and left them. They had a very snug little tract of land, but in the course of time they became embarrassed and had to pawn their land for money. They are now old and well stricken in years and ill able to labor. So their creditor could, I presume, any time he saw proper to push his debt, have them turned out of doors. Here, then, would be two fit subjects for public charity, such as, I presume, you could not find among the whole population of servants at the South. (I call them servants because I hate the name slave. The word slave is a borrowed term and should not be used.) Contrast the condition of the members of this family with bond servants of a like age, where they are under the protection of a kind, humane man as a master, and where they have servants to labor for them in their declining years, and tell me which you think is most happy.

The above family were the only free persons of color that lived immediately in my section, so I cannot be accused of being partial in selecting a case.

ANOTHER COMPARISON.

Again—it is argued by some that liberty is an inherent right; that we therefore have no right to deprive any people of their liberty, not even if their condition be bettered thereby. I will illustrate this by the following comparison, though simple, yet it will do to illustrate the point in question.

All will doubtless admit that the horse fares better in a domestic state than he would in his natural, or wild state where he could roam about at pleasure. Now, if these domestic

3

animals were liberated and turned out to shift for themselves, they would soon become subject to great want and suffering, and as a consequence, would pine away and die. Now, no person, I presume would argue, that for the sake of giving these brutes their liberty, this should be done. Even so with the negro. Though he does not need the fostering care of the white man to the same extent that the horse does, yet it is evident that he does to a certain degree, from the fact that he thrives better with it than without it.

ANOTHER COMPARISON.

The most menial services is, in many instances, the employment of free persons of color.

A few days back, as I was passing along E street, I heard a popping, banging and thrashing ahead of me, which I could not for my life conceive what it meant. Upon drawing nearer I discovered that it was a party of about a dozen negroes engaged dusting a carpet, each one with his stick laying on lustily. Then it seems if they be emancipated and allowed to remain among the whites, the most menial of services, more degrading than farm labor, would be their employment, and what is most to be feared is, they would not always get even enough of that to do. And if freed and put off to themselves, there would be danger of their going into barbarism and decay. Contrast their condition with that of bond servants, where they have plenty of work to do, plenty to eat, drink and wear, are kindly treated, and in old age well cared for.

ANOTHER COMPARISON AND THE LAST.

In conversation with emancipationists upon this subject, I have frequently been interrogated " *how would you like to be a slave?* " I will answer this by the following:

Suppose the Mayor of New York should propose to one of the merchant princes of that city to make him a policeman. The person thus addressed would doubtless take it as an insult. But were he to propose to one of the Irish laborers of the city to make him a policeman, he would doubtless accept the position gladly. The reason of the difference is obvious, because the employment which would be a degredation to the one, offers promotion and dignity to the other. In like manner, Slavery, to an individual of the Anglo-Saxon race, which occupies so high a rank in human estimation, would be a debasement not to be thought of with patience for a moment. And yet to the Guinea negro sunk in heathen barbarism, it would be a happy change to place him in the hands of a kind Southern master.

If men would reflect maturely on the subject, they would soon be convinced that liberty is a blessing to those, and only those, who are able to use it wisely. I will illustrate this by the following :

All waters are to a greater or less extent inhabited by fish. Even the waters of the mighty deep, although they are so salt that we can scarcely taste thereof, and much less support life therewith, are yet inhabited by immense multitudes of great and small fishes. Now, suppose we should conceive the idea, as fresh water is more agreeable to our taste, that the fish of the sea would also thrive better therein, and should transport some of them from thence to some fresh water course, what would be the consequence ? Why they would soon pine away and die. The sea is their natural element, and before removing them from thence it would be well for us to work upon them and change their natures, so as to make them conform to the new element, and if we fail to do this it would then be best for us to let them remain where they are. You will doubtless admit this.

I will here compare the servants at the South to the fishes of the sea. Whether or not they occupy their natural position, certain it is that it is one in which they have prospered more than any other in which they have ever yet been placed. Therefore, before changing their social position, we should first change their nature so as to make them conform to the new element. We need not argue that they should first be placed in the new element as they are, and let them conform thereto, for this experiment has been tried over and over again—the results of which I presume are generally known; and if we now try the experiment again under similar circumstances, similar results will be apt to follow. Therefore, before placing them in this new element their nature should first be changed and made to conform thereto; and if after a fair trial we fail to do this, I think you will admit that they had best remain as they are, after correcting the evils of servitude as much as possible.

I know the word master sounds badly to a great many— even to myself. I am therefore for consulting the interest of servants exclusively in this matter, and am for continuing them in servitude or not, according as their interest require. If this is not doing as we would be done by, I should like to know what is.

SOME MISCELLANEOUS ARGUMENTS—PROBABLE EFFECT OF EMANCIPATION.

A few words to emancipationists and I will soon conclude this already very lengthy article. As sensible men I beg you to pause and reflect, and consider well what you are doing. Listen to the words of one who has at heart the best interest of these people, ere perhaps a nation may be involved in irretrievable ruin. Have any of you proven that the negro would be better off emancipated than where he now is, under the protection of a good and kind man as a master. No, my friends, you have not done it; you cannot do it. And unless you can prove from the Scriptures,* and from

---

* If it could be clearly demonstrated that the condition of servants would be bettered by emancipation I believe it would be but little trouble to bring about general emancipation at the South. And it seems this

countries where emancipation has already taken place, that his condition would thereby be bettered, why do you wish to try the experiment on so large a scale? Before striking to free more of these people I would advise you to do something for those already freed and in your midst. It has already been shown that crime among the free negroes of Massachusetts, the State where they enjoyed freedom longer than those of any other State, is over thirteen times as great as among her white inhabitants. So if you desire to do something for these people, here is a field open for you. I will endeavor to make this plainer by the following illustration:

We will say that a master-workman gives an apprentice a job of work to do, and he instead of doing it well bungles over it in some way, or perhaps does a part of it wrong. He then applies to his master for more work. Does he give it to him? No, he tells him to go and do well the work that he gave him before, and he would then give him more. Even so in this case. Before you desire more work, first do well what you have on hand and you shall then have more.

Again: It is the belief of certain of your sect (emancipationists) that thorough abolition would tend to the extermination of the black race; that they would vanish under it as did the Indians from the presence of the white man. I have heard these words with my own ears; so I cannot be mistaken in making the assertion. Is this your belief also? If it is, I would advise you to desist. I don't believe God requires any such work at your hands. I don't believe He requires of you to sacrifice 1,000,000 human beings in order to place in the road for *extermination* 4,000,000 others. I positively do not envy the man his happiness that would advocate emancipation with such a belief as this.

should be the first step taken in the matter. So far as the people are concerned it is not so much the loss of their servants that causes them to oppose emancipationists, for a great many would voluntarily give them up if they thought they would be bettered by the change.

The negro is as yet but a child in intellect. I therefore think it should be our duty as Christian people to treat them kindly, and place them in whatever position they thrive best. I think the white race at least owes them that much ; for they were stolen from their homes in Africa and forced here against their will. Therefore, as we have plenty of room for them, and they can also occupy a useful position in society, why exterminate the poor creatures ?

It is, though, to be presumed that the above is a mere exception to the general rule, and that by far the larger portion of emancipationists inculcate their doctrine of universal freedom purely through philanthropic motives. But they have read Uncle Tom's Cabin and played it in their theatres away up North, until, in my opinion, they have formed many erroneous ideas concerning this institution.

MR. HELPER'S ERROR.

Again : If the owning of servants be such a monster of an evil, how is it that so few persons South, where they of all others have the best opportunities of seeing and judging for themselves, have been found to raise their voices against it ? We have, I presume, some as great philanthropists South as can be found anywhere else, and if this had been such a crime as is frequently represented, it seems that some of these would have come out and spoke against it. It is true a few have done this, and prominent among them was Mr. Helper, of North Carolina. But it is to be presumed that to better the condition of these people was not the object he had in view; as I have it from good authority that he hated negroes. The white man, then, seems to have been the object of his pseudo-philanthropy !

But suppose his object had been accomplished thoroughly— that all the servants had been emancipated—do you suppose the condition of the white man would have been bettered thereby ? No ; never a whit, as long as the South continued to overtrade to the North. He would then have found that he had been striking upon the wrong string altogether. For even if the servants had been emancipated, our merchants would still have continued to trade North as long as they could buy goods a few cents cheaper ; and while this state of affairs continued how could manufactories have been built up at the South ? For the Northern people having got their manufactories in successful operation, and having the channel of trade turned thither, and also selling such quantities, and running but little or no risk to effect sales for lack of custom, could, under these circumstances, sell cheaper than the Southern people. It was, therefore, to the advantage of the Southern merchant to trade North ; but it would, in the end, have been to the advantage of the people and community at large to have had at least a portion of these goods manufactured and vended at the South, even if they had for the time being been some higher. For I hold if I buy your corn, cotton, flour, &c., that you could then afford to buy of me my manufactured articles. By reciprocal trade the prices on both sides would soon be properly regulated. Therefore, to have a universally happy and prosperous country, all sections must produce as many of the necessary articles of home consumption as possible. Having somewhat digressed from the subject I will now return to it again.

WERE ALL MEN CREATED EQUAL?

I expect to adduce a few arguments to prove that all men were not created or born equal, and that the negro is an inferior species of the human race. But, even taking it for granted that they were not created equal, and that the negro is an inferior race, I, by no means, consider this a justifiable excuse for reducing them to bondage to serve a superior race, provided their pleasures and enjoyments of life would thereby be curtailed. I think, in this case, they should be looked upon with commiseration, and that it would be our duty as philanthropists to do something to elevate and better their condition, rather than to pounce upon them and sink them still lower in the scale of human existence, merely because nature happened to do a little more for us than it did for them. My only plea then, for retaining these people a day longer in servitude, is that, under existing circumstances, I don't think their condition would be bettered by changing their social position. I am for first applying to them the anointing oil of learning and christianity; and, whenever it shall have been clearly demonstrated that they are in a fit condition to take care of themselves, I am then for their going out free.

But if, after exhausting these means, it should be discovered that they had not made proper advances in the sciences and civilization, we might then fairly infer that God never intended that they should be placed on a level with the Caucasian or white race. I will now point out some of the principal features wherein the white and black races differ:

1st. They are born different anatomically considered. The white infant at birth has its brain enclosed by fifteen disunited bony plates. The negro infant is born with a hard, smooth, round head, like a gourd. The head of the negro infant is also smaller than that of the white.

2nd. The negro is a prognathos species of the human race, i. e. have receding foreheads. Prognathos is a technical term derived from *pro*, before, and *gnathos*, the jaws, indicating that the muzzle or mouth is anterior to the brain.

I could multiply these differences to a much greater extent, but think I have mentioned enough to prove conclusively that they do differ anatomically considered, and this difference too is of such a character as to indicate inferior intellectual endowments on the part of the black race. As a farther evidence of this, they thrive better in a state of servitude than in any other position in which they have ever yet been placed. Where the fetters of the white man have been broken they have, generally speaking, appreciated their liberties, and made advances in the arts, sciences, civilization and literature. But where the fetters of the black man have been broken they have, generally speaking, (I wish I could say otherwise,) made a retrograde movement, and started back for savagism, barbarism and mental decay.

Again. It appears singular that the words of Mr. Jefferson in the Declaration of Independence, " That all men were created equal," should be made to date back and apply as an interpretation of the Scriptures written by inspiration thousands and thousands of years before. No such doctrine is inculcated in the Scriptures, and it cannot be found within the lids of theBible that all men were created equal, such an idea being wholly of human origin.

In conclusion I would say, as certain emancipationists and philanthropists will probably differ with me in the views herein set forth, that I have written what I have solely as a duty, I think, I owe to my God, my country and my countrymen. And, as regards the colored people, I presume there is no person, neither North nor South, who has their interest at heart more than I; I sincerely wish them well. Therefore, before condemning what I have written relative thereto, I hope you will give the subject your careful consideration, and, if we still differ, let us differ honestly, and appeal to a decision of the people at the *ballot box* to say who is in the right.

THE TERRITORIAL QUESTION.

As the agitation of the slavery question, in connection with the territorial question, has had much to do in producing our present unhappy state of affairs, I deem it expedient to make a few remarks relative thereto.

The institution of slavery at the South was safe, and pro-

tected in the States where it existed ; and already the Southern people had more than twice as much land per head as
the Northern people, as I will show before I get through.
And more than this, the Missouri compromise line would
have given them far more than their just proportion of the
Territories, for rightly apportioned there was only about
one-fifth part of the Territories coming to the Southern people. But, not satisfied with this, thinking that Cotton was
King, their politicians thought they could sway things as
they pleased. (I presume they will find by the time these
sectional troubles are ended that Cotton is not King.) So,
by their machinations and thirst after power and revolution,
they managed to bring about a repeal of the Missouri Compromise, with the ostensible purpose of carrying slavery into
the Territories whithersoever they desired, thinking, it
seems, that they had a right to do as they pleased in this
matter, without consulting the non-slaveholders of the North
and the South.

In order to make this plainer I have made some calcula-
tions thereon, which are herewith submitted.

The population of the North in 1860 was 18,834,956.—
The population of the South was 12,254,849. The area of
the Northern States embraces 612,597 square miles—392,-
062,080 acres. This divided by 18,834,956 will give a little
over $20\frac{3}{4}$ acres to each person at the North.

The area of the Southern States embraces 851,508 square
miles—554,965,120 acres. This divided by 12,254,849 will
give a little over $44\frac{1}{4}$ acres to each person at the South. So,
before dividing the Territories, I think the North should
nave been made equal, or have had $23\frac{1}{2}$ acres thrown into
each inhabitant, so as to make her count $44\frac{1}{4}$ acres to each
person; then have divided the remainder according to ra-
tio of population. Let us see how this calculation will
figure. 18,834,956 multiplied by $23\frac{1}{2}$ will give 442,621,466
acres, equal to 691,596 square miles, that must first be as-

signed the North before the South should receive any more territory. This amount taken from 1,492,061 square miles, the amount now embraced in the Territories, will leave 800, 465 square miles to be divided between the North and the South. This would be in the proportion of about 1½ to the North and 1 to the South. Divided though accurately it would give 315,523 square miles to the South and 484,942 to the North; or, summing up the whole according to the plan already mentioned, the North would receive of the Territories 1,176,538 square miles ; the South 315,523 square miles. These lands divided in this way would give to each person North and South, with what they now have, about 60¾ acres. I will endeavor to make this some plainer.

The whole area of the Territories divided into States would make thirty of about the size of North Carolina. Of these the South would receive a little over six; the North the remainder. There would then be to each man, woman, and child, North and South, black and white, about 60½ acres of land as aforesaid. Therefore I think such a division would have been fair and just to both sections.

The people of England, Wales, Scotland, and Ireland have on an average a little less than three acres of land each. Those of Belgium, which I believe is the most densely populated country on the globe, have a little less than two. Were the United States settled as thickly as England, Wales, Scotland, and Ireland, instead of a population of 31,-000,000, we would have one of over 662,000,000 ; and were they settled as thickly as Belgium we would have a population of over 957,000,000. From these figures you may see that we had only made a beginning towards developing our vast resources.

In order that I may not be misunderstood I will remark that I am not for giving the North the amount of land mentioned in order to make her count numerically equal with the South, but let them be divided according to the plan already given, and let the people of each section pay into the Treasury the market value thereof as they are taken up.

I will further state that the 315,523 square miles falling to the South should be subdivided into slave and free territory after the following plan: Let the people at the South all vote and represent their respective families whether they would have their portion of these Territories slave or free. Thus, if a man have a wife and ten children let his vote count numerically twelve. If he have a wife, ten children, and twenty servants, let his vote count numerically thirty-two. Thus the business would be so arranged that by all the people voting the number of votes cast would be equal to the whole number of people at the South, bond and free, (12,254,849.) I am aware that many people at the South would vote for free territory, and I think they have as good a right so to vote as the slaveholders have to vote for slave territory, and thus scatter slavery over every foot of Southern soil. I think it is of no advantage neither to the servants nor their owners to scatter them over such a large expanse of country, but rather the reverse.

If the slaveholders were allowed to represent their servants numerically, they ought to be satisfied therewith, and I think they would be. The portion of the Territories that would thus fall to the South would average a little over sixteen acres to each individual; and I think the non-slaveholder should have the same right to say that his portion shall be free territory that the slaveholder has to say that his portion shall be slave territory. I not only think this plan fair and just, but that it should have been inaugurated sooner, even soon after the admission of Texas, and let that State have been divided into slave and free territory, had the people of the South seen fit to do so. I think in this division the black race should be represented to their full numerical value; for, though they are black, it takes as much land to support a black man as it does a white man, and I therefore think they should receive their full distributive share thereof.

I think the territorial and slavery questions should be settled, and settled permanently. Have no more voting upon them. At these elections, when a State is to be admitted into the Union, with or without slavery, as the case may be, there is always too much excitement at them, too apt to be blood spilt; and the excitement thus got up extends throughout both sections, and it is not to be wondered at that much trouble should have grown out thereof. Therefore, let this danger be avoided in the future by settling these questions fairly, permanently, and forever. Had the Southern people struck for a compromise upon some such terms . as the foregoing, I have not a doubt but the business might have been settled fairly and permanently. But, instead of doing this, they have come out under the protection of State laws, and have assailed the best government the world ever saw. Our Government, though good, had some defects in it; but it should have been our duty to remedy these defects, and not have disrupted the Union for trivial causes, and in place of the lesser evils have brought on others infinitely greater.

Let the interest of servants be which way it may, if the rebels of the South persist long enough in this wicked, unholy, and uncalled-for war, slavery will certainly be wiped out as a consequence of the war, if nothing else. So, let what will become of slavery, in the language of the patriotic Jackson, " The Union must and shall be preserved."

WHY THE REBELLION HAS NOT BEEN SUPPRESSED SOONER.

It has doubtless been looked upon with wonder and astonishment by the Northern people, as well as Unionists South, how the Southern people, under such great disadvantages, have been able to hold out so long. The population of the Northern States exceeds that of the Southern more than two

to one if we except the servants of the latter. And besides
this the States of Delaware, Maryland, Virginia, Kentucky,
Missouri Tennesee and Arkansas, have sent, I believe,
111 regiments of soldiers to the field to fight against
the rebellion. In addition to this the North have a large
and powerful fleet, and the Southern people as good as none.
There is also an extensive Union sentiment in the States of
North Carolina,* Georgia and Alabama, which has troubled

---

* In order to give some idea of the Union sentiment in my section I will
give the vote of two counties, Randolph and Moore, (the former being my
native county, but I subsequently removed to the latter,) that was cast
for and against the Convention, on the 28th day of February, 1861.

Randolph, out of a vote of 2,600 cast for the Convention only 24; Moore,
out of 1,300 cast for the Convention 68. Adding these together and making an average, we find that secession was voted down in the two counties by more than 40 to 1. I quote from memory and may, perhaps, have
underrated the Union vote a little, but think I quote the secesh vote accurately. So it is to be wondered at how this large Union element could
ever be made subservient to the secesh authorities. But when the law
gets against the people they can't do much. For an organized force can
swallow up and make subservient one unorganized many times larger.
But the masses of the people still remain the same. For they look upon
it that the causes were not justifiable for secession, and much less for this
wicked war ; and, if wrong in the beginning, that fighting can never make
it right, though there be ever so much blood spilt. The masses of the
people love the old Government, and gladly would they return to their
former allegiance if they had it in their power. Not but the Union forces
were right in attacking the rebs, for what else could they do when the
United States flag had been fired upon and outraged at three different times
before a shot was returned, and this, rather than secession, may be considered as the cause of the war. But still if President Lincoln had resorted
to a little strategy, as follows, it is thought he would have killed secession
as dead as a hammer without firing a gun, and that is, let him soon after
his inauguration have issued a proclamation to the Southern people in
effect as follows :

*To the Governors and people of the States of Delaware, Maryland, Virginia,
North Carolina, South Carolina, Georgia, Alabama, Mississippi, Louisi-
ana, Florida, Texas, Tennessee, Kentucky, Missouri, and Arkansas :*

My countrymen: It is with regret that I see a cloud gathering, which,
if not arrested, may soon culminate, break over our heads, and disperse

the Confederate authorities much in the prosecution of the war. So, when we take all these things into consideration, it is much to be wondered at how the rebels have been enabled to hold out so long. This can only be accounted for in one way. The Federal army attacking and failing to carry their point at some of the rebel strong holds, instead of attacking them at some of the weaker and more vulnerable places, where important victories could easily have been gained and at, comparatively speaking, but little loss, to-

---

all our prosperity of former days. I have been elected as President of the people, and it is my determination to serve you as such ; desiring to treat you as near like Washington, Jefferson, and Madison did, as I can, I shall therefore know no North, no South, no East, no West. I will also state that I have no desire nor intention of interfering with any of your local institutions whatever. Therefore, as one whose bosom beats with a fervent desire for the welfare of my country and countrymen, I do declare emphatically that there shall be no blood spilt during my administration, if I can help it. But, believing that you have in seceding acted more through fear of apprehended dangers than from any other cause, I have, in order that I may dispel this fear, clearly and explicitly set forth my views, which are likewise the views of my party that elected me to office, and now, desiring the opinion of the Southern people in reference thereto, I do hereby issue this my proclamation, desiring that the legal voters of all the aforesaid States (for you are all interested alike) shall assemble at their respective places of holding elections, on the —— day of —— next, and cast their votes whether or not they wish to secede for existing causes.

In order that this may be made more effective, I enjoin upon the Governors of the aforesaid States to issue their proclamations, ordering the convening of the people of their respective States, on the day and for the purposes above specified. Should any of the States vote by a majority to secede, I could not of myself give them up, but would shortly convene Congress to consider the matter.

If the President had issued a proclamation to the effect of the above, secession would, in my opinion, have been killed so dead that it would scarcely have been known to have had any existence. For, in my opinion, there is not a State at the South in which the ordinance would not have been killed, could the people have voted fairly upon it, and, in the most of the States by overwhelming majorities. And in case the Governors of some of the States that had already seceded had not seen fit to submit this gether with the dissentions among the Northern people, have, in my opinion, tended more to prolong the war than any other two causes.

I will give an illustration of this. A few days before the seven day's fight before Richmond took place, I was in Wilmington, N. C., and heard the citizens of that place say, that for the Federals to take that city they had but to come after it. At that time the Southern people had such a perfect horror of a gunboat that I don't suppose there would have

------

ordinance to a popular vote of the people, there would have been such opposition gotten up thereto on the part of the people, that it would have been a dead-go anyway. Therefore, even in this sense of the word, the rebellion could never have gained much headway. For, even if the secessionists had tried to do anything, the words of the President would have come up before them, and they would soon have cowered down into insignificance. That strategy would have had a good effect, I will illustrate by the following :

We are informed that the historian Josephus upon a certain occasion condemned a criminal to have both his hands cut off. At this he began to bemoan, and besought Josephus that he would at least spare him one of his hands, to which he assented. The criminal then submitted for one to be taken off with but little regret. But it was a ruse on the part of Josephus, to get it willingly, he not intending to take but one at the start.

Strategy here was of benefit, and a little on the part of the President, it is thought, would have averted these evils from the country ; or, at all events, would have shortened the war much if we had had one.

But after coercion was attempted on the part of the General Government, the secessionists used all manner of devices to increase their army, saying "The Yanks are going to take your lands and homes to pay the expenses of the war ; they will also free the negroes, and have them in your midst, walking with and intermarrying your daughters," and all such like. So the harder they were pressed upon the more force they could bring out. This may be likened unto a bridge that Julius Cæsar built, upon a certain occasion. It was so constructed that the harder the waters pressed against it so much the more firmly were the timbers bound together. Even so with the rebellion. Under milder treatment, it is thought the fabric would have dissolved, and floated down the current of time long ago, or rather, could never have been built up.

In view also of the large Union sentiment in many sections at the South,

been a gun fired, or at least that was the talk of the citizens of the place. Therefore, if the Union forces had only made a feint upon Richmond and had gone round and have taken Wilmington and other vulnerable places, how much they would have been worth to the Union cause! If Wilmington had been taken at that time North Carolina would have been compelled to come back into the Union ere this, be-. cause she could not possibly have supplied her citizens with

---

the thing should be viewed with as much allowance as possible. The woods or the army was the alternative ; and a man, unless he have con׳ siderable means, can't exist in the woods two years. If Governor Brown, of Georgia, had not made that mistake when he refused to let his militia officers go in the army, by which means a regularly organized force was left behind to hunt down and harrass poor conscripts and deserters, the rebellion would, in my opinion, have been played out long ago. I will take occasion to say here, that had the people of my section been near enough the Union forces to join them, that there would to-day be far more of them fighting under the stars and stripes than there are under the rebel flag. I will also state that I believe, if the Union forces would now hold off a little and not make any more advances at present, and hold out the olive branch of peace, that time, through the depreciation of their currency South, and enormously high prices of provisions, would effect a reunion as soon, if not sooner, than more forcible measures. For it is evident that the North cannot conquer and overrun the whole South ; and I think they now have in their possession as much as they can hold to advantage. And if they would now fortify these points, hold their own, and not be in too big a hurry, and be satisfied to give a little time, I think peace and reunion would soon be the consequence. The reason that I speak thus is because I know the sentiments of many of the Southern people, and know that they desire peace and reunion, and without any farther shedding of blood. Therefore, all that is wanting is for the Anaconda that has been placed about their necks to be loosed, and let them speak out—and time, I think, would do this more effectually than more forcible means. For when you attack them, this immense serpent draws his coils more closely around them, and thus presses more men into the service. But if suffered to remain inactive awhile, he would unloose his coils, and thus to a certain extent release the people. You could then get more aid from Unionists South. Therefore

> All you that by hard fighting would excel,
> How much you fight regard not, but how well.

4

salt. Large quantities of this were manufactured in and around Wilmington, which sold at from forty to fifty cents per pound, and was scarcely to be had at that in sufficient quantities to supply the wants of the people. Therefore, if Wilmington had fallen, North Carolina would soon have fallen also, and one star plucked from the Confederacy the remaining States would soon have followed. And the beauty of the thing is that all of this might have been accomplished with but little or no loss of life.

The failure of the Union forces to take Richmond at that time was probably owing as much to their having undertaken an impossibility under existing circumstances, as to anything else; for the whole Southern Confederacy was there, so to speak. Already there were a great many troops at Richmond, but for several days before the battle every train by Raleigh and Wilmington was loaded down to the full with soldiers "for Richmond." Therefore, if there had been a little strategy used at this time the rebellion would, in my opinion, have been played out long ago, and at a great saving of life also.

It is also thought by some that the emancipation policy has had a bad, rather than a good, effect, and that, if it's farther enforcement was withheld, say for ninety days, so as to give the rebs one more chance, and would then call for volunteers, that the road leading to a restoration of the Union would be as plain as the road to market. I will remark that so far as I am concerned, I would be for the emancipation policy if I thought the Union would thereby be restored sooner, and at a saving of life and treasure. In fact, I am for any just and honorable means leading to this end, and am, therefore, for using the negroes in any way that they can aid in putting down the rebellion, by which their condition would not be permanently worsted. And that they can aid materially in this business, even without going into the army, there is no doubt. It is, therefore, evident, if the

South have to be brought back by 'orce of arms alone, that the emancipation policy would have been the thing, provided the North had hung together on this question. But, taking that into consideration, together with the extensive Union sentiment in many portions of the South, it is thought some milder means would probably have done as well.

It is also thought that a reunion, to be worth anything, must be based upon the will of the people governed, and that, therefore, to have a good and permanent Government the extremists North and South must yield, and let the question at issue be decided by a popular vote of the people.

REV. DR. MASSIE, OF ENGLAND, VISITS THE UNITED STATES.

I think it was in June, of the present year, that the Rev. Dr. Massie, of England, visited the United States. He brought with him a petition signed by some seven hundred and fifty Protestant Ministers of France, and some five thousand of those of England, for the purpose of furthering the emancipation policy, which he presented to the President and Cabinet. If these gentlemen could do anything calculated to restore peace and quietude to our bleeding country, most happy would we be for them to do so. But anything that is calculated to embitter the feelings, prolong the struggle, and thus make the breach between the two sections greater, we do not desire to see. We, therefore, think that when the services of these Reverend gentlemen are needed to interpose in our political affairs they should be notified thereof.

THE REBELLION WANING.

It is to be presumed that the Administration have resorted to no means for the prosecution of this unnatural and uncalled-for war on the part of the rebs, only such as was thought would be instrumental in restoring the Union and at a saving of life and treasure. Therefore, if any of these measures have turned out to be impolitic, we should take it into consideration that this could not be known until they had been tried.

The rebels have tried certain impolitic measures, and prominent among them was the law exempting the owner of, or person having in charge, twenty negroes. This was about to work a considerable disturbance in placing a distinction between the slave and non-slave holder. Their legislators seeing this, wisely for the cause of the rebellion, repealed the ordinance before any serious disturbance had grown out thereof.

But be the emancipation ordinance and certain military changes that have been made, politic or impolitic measures, I think we have now got to where we can see through the rebellion. Therefore, if we will pull together, pull steadily, and hold out faithful a little while longer, the stars and stripes will, as I believe, soon wave triumphantly throughout the entire length and breadth of the land.

WE MUST KEEP UNITED.

But in order to attain to this great desideratum it is expedient that we keep united at this the most important period in our national existence, or we may yet, perhaps, through the dissensions and divisions of the people, lose the prime object for which the Union forces set out, after having borne the burden and heat of the day. Then all the fighting that has been done, and the much blood that has been spilt on the part of the Union forces, will all have been spilt in vain.— The stars and stripes, the flag of the nation, would go down with dishonor and disgrace, and another be built upon the ruins thereof. Shall we thus, through dissensions, be compelled to acknowledge the independence of the South, and thus, in effect, acknowledge that they were right in seceding when the causes were not justifiable? Acknowledge that they were right in firing upon and capturing Fort Sumpter, when it might have been honorably avoided? Acknowledge that they were right in inaugurating this cruel civil war, in which seas of blood have been poured out and billions of treasure expended? Acknowledge that those who have had 'treasonable intents against the General Government for the last thirty or forty years, were right at length in putting them forth? Acknowledge all these things, and, above all, permit those secessionists to build up a government based upon usurped power and against the will of a majority of the people at the South? No! never, never! Never will I, for one, as long as breath animates my body and while there is even a remote chance for success, agree to this.

If we would not have all these evils, and even greater, to come upon us, we must keep united. Justice to liberty, our country and our God demand that we keep united. Justice to the gallant dead who have fallen in defence of the stars and stripes, and who now lay mouldering in the clay, demand that we keep united. Justice to the many loyal people South, who have held out amidst various trials and persecutions, and who still hold out with the hope, in the end, of seeing the stars and stripes wave triumphantly over them, demand that we keep united. We must keep united or all may yet be lost, irretrievably lost.

The Southern people are principally building their hopes of success upon the prospect of these dissensions and a consequent revolution among the Northern people. This I know. Therefore, if the people would now exhaust this source of aid and comfort by becoming united, the rebellion would, and, as I believe, with but very little more shedding of blood, vanish like a bank of snow before a summer's sun.

We will take it for granted that the *status* or standing of the General Government towards the seceded States has only been changed in such things as they were driven to by the acts of the secessionists. This is but fulfilling the Scriptures where it says "one evil word calleth for another." We will, therefore, take it for granted, as soon as the rebellion shall have been conquered, that the former *status* or standing of the General Government will be resumed, unless a majority of the people should say otherwise. Therefore, it would be better for us to yield our private opinions for the present, than to cleave thereto and thereby endanger the Union cause. For we should recollect, in proportion as we divide and relax our energies North, that in just this same proportion do we give aid and comfort to the rebellion South. We should, therefore, know no party at this most important crisis, "save the Union and it saved." This sentiment should rise paramount to every party consideration. We should, therefore, be willing to leave these questions of minor importance for the people to decide hereafter, as they would, doubtless, decide them *right*. Therefore, keep united, press forward, don't give up the ship, and when it gets too hot for our Southern brethren let them come back into the Union where they ought to be, and from which, in my opinion, they ought never to have gone. And, having gone without a cause, they may at last blame themselves most for the many privations, hardships and sufferings they now endure.. And should slavery eventually suffer, they may also blame themselves most for that; for they were warned and told in time that secession would in all probability lead to the emancipation of their servants·

TO MY SOUTHERN COUNTRYMEN.

The following is, in the main, intended for my Southern brethren, should it by chance fall into their hands:

MY DEAR FRIENDS:—What have your politicians and the secessionists promised you? They promised you that it should be peaceable secession. Some in their speeches asserted that they would pay the cost of the war for ten cents; others that they would wipe up all the blood that would be spilt with a pocket handkerchief; and others still more generous, said they would agree to drink all the blood that would be spilt. To be short, they by making such speeches as the above, managed to deceive many of you, and to get you to volunteer, telling you that we must present a formidable front, and thus back out the North. Whether or not, these persons were conscientious in making these statements, I am unable to say, but if they were certain, it is, that it has turned out, that they were greatly mistaken. After getting a goodly number of you to volunteer, they soon got the war started, and after getting that started, they soon devised means for forcing the remainder of you into the army. They did this first by the draft, and then subsequently and more completely by the unjust conscription. Even those of you, who had been bitterly opposed to secession and its fruits from the start, and whom they had denied the just rights of freemen in not permitting you to vote directly upon this all-important subject, they now, by their unjust legislation, compelled to take up arms, and go forth and fight the battles of the war that they had themselves inaugurated, sometimes even hunting you down, casting you in prison, and sending you forth in irons to shed your blood upon some cruel battle field. Was it justice, that you as peaceable citizens should thus have been hunted down, torn from your innocent and dependent families, and compelled to go forth and enact scenes that were revolting to your feelings, revolting to christianity, and revolting to civilization? Was it justice that our politicians largely in the minority, should thus of their own arbitrary power legislate away, as it were, your lives, and thereby create desolation, ruin and mourning throughout the entire length and breadth of the land? It undoubtedly was not justice, and to sum up the whole in a few words, was in my opinion, a grand usurpation of power, and ought not to have been submitted to for a moment.

I think in all republican governments, a majority of the people should rule, and particularly upon these all important questions like the present, which has involved us in so much trouble and distress. Therefore, as our politicians thought proper to bring on this war without consulting you, I now think it would be fair and just for you to end the war without consulting them by deserting and fleeing from them, and leaving those secessionists to fight their own battles if they want any fought. Yea, I think your outraged rights demand that you should speedily desert and flee from them like rats from a sinking ship, and let the structure founder, and go down with the secesh only on board should they choose to hold on, and the next time they wish to secede, let them consult the masses of the people.

A FEW WORDS IN MY OWN DEFENCE.

I have by these sectional troubles been compelled to take one of three positions, which were: first to take sides with m*y* Southern brethren in the rebellion ; second, espouse the Union cause; and third, remain neutral, which I could easily have done after getting rid of the conscription.

But I could not take sides with my Southern brethren in the rebellion, from the fact, that I did not think the causes justified secession. And when so many of my fellow men were fast passing from time to eternity, feeling that I had a duty to perform, I could not content myself to remain neutral. Therefore, believing that my Southern brethren acted with too much haste, first, in seceding, and then inaugurating this wicked war ; and, also, believing that the only safe and permanent way of settling our difficulties, is by a restoration of the Union, I have considered it my imperative duty to espouse the Union cause, and vindicate its principles through weal and through woe.

But I have thus been placed in a very uncomfortable situation, for I have kindred, persons that are near and dear to me by the ties of nature in the Southern army, and oh! shall they go down, or shall I once more, in peace, be permitted to behold their happy faces ? This is a subject that draws like chords around my heart, and nothing but a conscientious belief, that I was in the discharge of my duty would have prompted me to have taken the stand that I have. Yea, before I would have done anything in this matter that I conceived would be against the best interest of my Southern brethren, and country generally, I would have suffered the last drop of blood that is within my veins to run cold. But it being a matter of so very great importance, one in which the very life of our country, as well as the destinies of probably many future generations is involved, I considered it my imperative duty to espouse the Union cause, and stand by it, live or die, sink or swim. I have accordingly done this at much expense and great risk. At length for issuing and circulating certain *publications, I was twice arrested and imprisoned, and being in danger of a third arrest for a similar offense, thinking it might not go so well with me, as I had been told I would be tried for treason if arrested any more, I deemed it expedient to evade this by crossing the line, and did so. I am though glad to see that free speech is once more becoming dominant in my native State. Old North Carolina will soon take her position once more under the stars and stripes, and one star plucked from the Confederacy, the remaining States would soon follow.

PLAN FOR RESTORING THE UNION.

Before closing, I wish to give a plan by which I think the Union can be restored, and at comparatively little loss of life. I have endeavored to show that there is an extensive Union sentiment existing in various portions of the South. Measures that would now increase this sentiment would, in my opinion, be the plan. And, in my opinion, the best way for doing this would be to give them evidence that a strong conservative feeling exists North. And the best way to test this would be to submit the following resolution to the legal voters of all the free States, and let them vote thereon, for or against as they see proper ; to wit:

" That this war is not waged on their part in any spirit of

oppression, or for the purpose of overthrowing or interfering with the rights and established institutions of the States, but to defend and maintain the supremacy of the Constitution, and to preserve the Union with all the dignity, equality, and rights of the several States unimpaired, and that as soon as these objects are accomplished the war ought to cease,"

If the above were submitted to the Northern people, and an extensive Union sentiment should thereby be shown forth, I believe it would have more effect in restoring peace and a reunion than all the gunpowder in the United States. And if thus restored by conciliatory measures, the work would then be completed. We could then join together and journey on once more happily and prosperously together. But if restored solely by force of arms, conciliatory measures would at last have to be resorted to; for, as has already been said, "A reunion, to be worth anything, must be based upon the will of the people governed." I therefore think the Union could be restored sooner, and at a greater saving of human life, by this plan, than by any other known to me. Or it might be so arranged as to have a proposition submitted to the Southern people also; and that is, let the two Governments by mutual agreement come to the understanding that, if the proposition already mentioned were submitted to the people of the Northern States, and should be carried favorably, that the Confederate authorities should then submit to the Southern people the question whether or not they would accept a reunion upon this basis. If we could thus get this question out of the hands of the politicians into those of the people, I think they would soon decide it, and decide it right.

It is also thought, as the Federal Government is vastly superior in strength and power, that the Administration could, without endangering the cause in the least, either submit or receive proposals leading to peace and conciliation. I have so much confidence in the above plan that if it could be inaugurated I would be willing to risk my all, even my life, that it would result in a restoration of the Union.

But if force of arms alone be resorted to, the longer our sectional troubles remain unsettled the more new difficulties will spring up, and the harder it will be in the end to reconcile them. We need not expect to settle our difficulties, and particularly by force of arms, in such a way as to be satisfied immediately at the result ; for, let us settle them as we may, it will take time, and a great deal of it at that, to effectually heal the awful breach that has been made. Many times, if we would do what is best, we must do things that we do not wish to do. So of this all-important subject, now before us. Let us consult our interest rather than our feelings, for it is a subject in which is involved the destinies of probably many future generations ; and if such a subject as this will not justify our yielding in some of our mere personal feelings, I should like to know one that would. So before tearing up and consigning to utter desolation and ruin this once fair portion of the earth, let us make one mighty effort to restore peace and quietude to our now disaffected country by conciliatory measures. *But if in the end mild words and gentle means would not reclaim the wicked, they must then be dealt with in a more severe manner.*

CONCLUSION.

I have endeavored to give my views impartially upon this all-important subject, and we now come to take our last view of the matter. But, before doing so, I would desire to urge upon you, my countrymen, the vast importance of the struggle in which we are now engaged. The destinies of unborn generations are depending upon the issue. We should therefore rise up in our might, and declare that the Union must and shall be preserved. Had our forefathers been here, do you suppose they would have disrupted the Union for the causes that existed at the commencement of our sectional troubles? No ; never, never. A voice from our gallant dead, who had fallen in the achievement of our liberties, and who now lay mouldering in a common grave, would have come up before them, saying, "Down with your schisms and divisions. It was not for this that we fought, bled, and died. Keep united, and you will be a great, happy, and prosperous people."

Therefore, the difficulties between the North and the South should not be viewed as existing between foreign enemies, but between people that should be towards each other as brothers, both sides of which have erred and gone aside from the path of duty. If each side would now do away with these wrongs, and let the two sections be united upon just and honorable terms, will, I think, in the end, be for the best.

Shall the Monarchal Powers of Europe point to our country as an example and say, that man is incapable of self-government? I hope not. Let us then join together as erring brothers, and yet solve the problem "that man is capable of self-government." What do you think the Father of his country would say were he now back to take a view of his once beloved country? "United we stand: divided we fall," would probably be his words.

We were making onward and upward strides, and the United States, but for these sectional troubles were destined soon to have taken the front rank among the nations of the globe. But oh! where are we now? I answer in the broad road that leads to ruin, speeding our way thither, as fast as the wheels of time impelled forward by the rage of an infuriated people, can bid us fly.

Oh! that those that were principally in fault, in bringing on our sectional troubles, may soon be brought to see their error, and that their course may be changed before it be everlasting too late; that the dark cloud which has lowered over us as a nation and people, may soon break away; and that peace, ah! blessed peace, may beam forth upon us; and that we may ere long be a united, contented, and happy people, is the sincere desire of one who has at heart the interest of both sections of the country.